D1125788

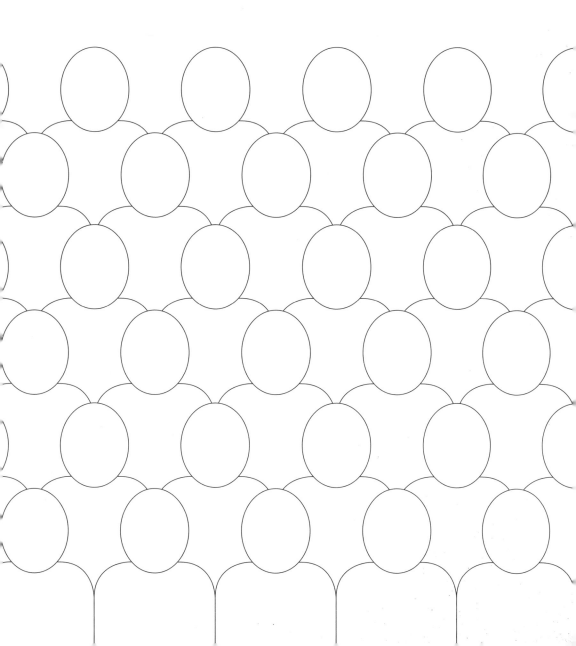

"For a graphic designer, whose whole life revolves around controlling the nuances, it is a bit scary to do something, to put it out there, and to have other people screwing around with it. But you get over it really quickly, because it turns out to be so much fun."

—STEFAN G. BUCHER

"I'm interested
in trying to
understand what
those conditions
are that allow
people to feel that
they're invited to
participate in your
work, either as
its producers or as
audience members."

—KATIE SALEN

"I think that I'm more of a gardener than an architect. I much prefer to plant something and see how it grows. I think that's why we work with live data flows. The world itself is so much more interesting than any logo I could come up with, or any color choice that I might make."

—ERIC RODENBECK

Fresh Dialogue Eight / New Voices in Graphic Design

Designing Audiences

With a foreword by Emma Presler

Princeton Architectural Press
American Institute of Graphic Arts New York Chapter
New York, 2008

Published by
Princeton Architectural Press
37 East Seventh Street
New York, New York 10003

For a free catalog of books, call 1.800.722.6657.
Visit our website at www.papress.com.

AIGA/NY
164 Fifth Avenue
New York, New York 10010
www.aiga.org

Mission

EXCLUSIVE/INCLUSIVE	THE MISSION OF AIGA/NY
DEBATE/DISCUSS	IS TO IDENTIFY AND DEFINE ISSUES
YOU/US	CRITICAL TO ITS MEMBERSHIP
BUSINESS/COMMUNITY	AND THE GRAPHIC DESIGN PROFESSION
RANTS/RAVES	TO EXPLORE AND CLARIFY THESE ISSUES
PROFITABLE/SUSTAINABLE	FOR THE PURPOSE OF HELPING TO ELEVATE
	THE STANDARDS OF THE BUSINESS
ART/COMMERCE	OF GRAPHIC DESIGN
DOGMATIC/PRAGMATIC	AND TO CREATE A FORUM FOR THE EXCHANGE OF
	INFORMATION, VIEWS, IDEAS AND TECHNIQUES
US/YOU	AMONG THOSE ENGAGED IN THE PROFESSION.

Fresh Dialogue Chair: Emma Presler
Editor: Nicola Bednarek
Designers: Jan Haux and Deb Wood

Special thanks to: Nettie Aljian, Sara Bader, Dorothy Ball, Janet Behning,
Kristin Carlson, Becca Casbon, Penny (Yuen Pik) Chu, Russell Fernandez,
Pete Fitzpatrick, Wendy Fuller, Clare Jacobson, John King, Aileen Kwun,
Nancy Eklund Later, Linda Lee, Aaron Lim, Laurie Manfra, Katharine Myers,
Lauren Nelson Packard, Jennifer Thompson, Arnoud Verhaeghe, Paul Wagner,
and Joseph Weston of Princeton Architectural Press
—Kevin C. Lippert, publisher

Library of Congress Cataloging-in-Publication Data is available from the
publisher.

Contributors:

Stefan G. Bucher

Katie Salen

Eric Rodenbeck

Moderator:

Ze Frank

Date:

29 May 2007

Location:

Fashion Institute of Technology

Contents:

Foreword
by Emma Presler

Fresh Dialogue
Chair 2007

Board member and
Secretary, AIGA/NY
2006–2008

In this year's installment of Fresh Dialogue we decided to reinvigorate the notions of "fresh" and "dialogue" in our choice of theme and speakers. For the past twenty-three years, the goal of the Fresh Dialogue program has remained unchanged. The event aims to expose the New York design community to the new and the different, bringing emergent ideas in design to light before they become full-blown trends. In keeping with this tradition, Khoi Vinh, my colleague and fellow board member, proposed a smart and timely theme that has resonance and relevance to a wide range of designers. Historically, graphic designers have been seen as storytellers, crafters of visual narratives designed for mass consumption. Now, that paradigm of design as controlled narrative is undergoing a seismic shift. Design is increasingly being valued as a facilitator of conversations where author and audience share control in multivariant experiences. In this new user-centric world where Nike iD, Flickr, and YouTube rule the roost, how does the role of the designer change? The event title, "Designing Audiences," intentionally lets the double entendres stand to help underscore the symbiotic nature of this shifted paradigm.

It is a shift that is at once profound and subtle, as is often the case with the new, the different, and the emergent. Sometimes it seems as if the only practitioners who can actualize this ambitious trifecta are those young and energetic enough to constantly experiment, unwittingly pushing the boundaries of a design cannon they may or may not know exists. As a result, "fresh" has become synonymous with "young," giving rise to the perception that the truly new in design is the exclusive purview of those in a certain age bracket. While this year's participants may not fall into that nascent category, their work reflects the same untarnished excitement that is borne out of grid-skipping across design categorizations and designations, sometimes

12

with wild abandon. They have all adopted an operational crossover that has become the hallmark of a genre that is still in its infancy. We wanted to honor their explorations and hard-won optimism in an event that would be simultaneously entertaining, visually sumptuous, and intellectually stimulating.

We felt it was imperative that designers in different media engage these questions. Stefan G. Bucher comes from a print design background and has recently entered the online world with his Daily Monster series where he brings pen-and-ink illustrations to a participatory audience. Katie Salen is a game designer whose most recent project, Karaoke Ice, challenges our preconceived perceptions of what experience design means. Eric Rodenbeck of Stamen Design operates in the online arena of live data visualization where he erases all apparent contradictions between visual beauty and sophisticated technology. All three have managed to redefine that joyous, contentious relationship between design and its consumers in their respective fields.

We knew this heady discussion would need the masterful guidance of someone accessible, highly knowledgeable in the subject and, hopefully, entertaining. Ze Frank fulfilled all of these criteria as our moderator and then some. Equal parts online impresario and stand-up comic, he is also creator of The Show and a soon-to-go-Hollywood charmer. He is intimately familiar with the challenges of designing in what I have termed "the era of constant feedback." He is also savvy enough to make the pitfalls seem manageable and the rewards worthwhile because he has successfully negotiated both in his work.

The twenty-third Fresh Dialogue proved to be a rich meditation on exactly what designing audiences entails, implies, and demands. This book documents that discussion.

Background conversation
. . .
Enter Emma Presler

EMMA PRESLER: Hello everyone and welcome to Fresh Dialogue. It is my pleasure to introduce Ze Frank, your moderator and host for tonight's program. Ze Frank is an online performance artist, composer, humorist, and public speaker. In 2001 he created an online birthday invitation called "How to Dance Properly" and sent it to seventeen of his closest friends. Forwarded wildly, the invitation soon generated millions of hits and over 100 gigabytes of daily web traffic to Ze's personal website. His site has grown to include interactive group projects, short films, animations, and video games. Ze won a 2002 Webby Award for Best Personal Web Site and was featured in Time magazine's Fifty Coolest Web Sites in 2005. He debuted on stage at the Gel Conference of 2003 and spoke at the Ted Conference in both 2004 and 2005. In March of 2006, he launched a daily video blog known simply as The Show with Ze Frank. Each tightly edited three-to-five-minute episode combined Daily Show–style commentary on world events with songs, observations, and occasionally games or challenges for his viewers to participate in. The Show has quickly become the most popular portion of his site. Ze has also served as an adjunct professor at New York University, Parsons The New School for Design, and SUNY Purchase. So please join me in welcoming Ze.

Applause

Background conversation

Enter Ze Frank

15

ZE FRANK: Thank you. Before introducing the people who you're really here to see, I'd first like to give you an idea of why I'm on this stage. We just heard about my "How to Dance Properly" invitation,[1] which really was my entrance into the issue of "Designing Audiences." So what happened exactly? I filmed myself dancing to Madonna's "Justify My Love," uploaded the video to my website as part of an invitation to my twenty-ninth birthday party, and sent the link out to seventeen of my closest friends on a Thursday.

By the following Monday, over a million people visited the site a day. Every single time I checked my email, messages were flooding in. On Wednesday I got a call from my credit card company asking me to authorize a $30,000 overage charge, based on ten cents a megabyte overage. I hadn't slept in four days. And my friends asked, "Why don't you just shut it off?" I said, "Shut it off? People are finally paying attention to me!"

I was addicted to web traffic at this point. I had never experienced this massive invisible audience and I wanted to figure out how to keep it. So I did what anyone probably would have done: copy myself. I used the same crappy navigation that I had thrown together in a half hour for the birthday invitation and the same sort of short video films, but the people just left, they weren't staying

[1]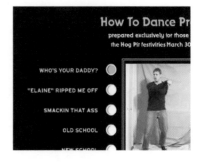

16

around. I tried again and eventually started using my cat in my videos, but I think using your pets is a sure sign that you're running out of ideas.[2]

So I asked myself, "What about all those emails I received? Maybe I can start mining them for ideas." For example, I got an email that said, "Dear Ze, can you make me a talking frog?"[3] I said, "Yes, absolutely." "No, no, no, no, no." Somebody else asked, "Can you make me a dancing puppet?" "Yes, absolutely."

Sings

Rap music

Another person wrote that I needed more games on my site, so I made a fully customizable game, where you jump around, with collision detection and so on. All in all, I had developed a very simple way of interacting with the audience, which was basically using them as a source of inspiration. But I was still doing all the work.

This was around the time the great fracture of Web 2.0 happened online, when the Internet became part publishing platform, part something else—you could either do the work yourself or have the audience do it and then take credit for it.

Laughs

Now, the focus of Web 2.0 is something called consumer-created, or citizen-created content—in other words, crap-o-copia, or the content for which there appears to be no sustainable revenue model.

Consumer-created content has actually been out there for quite a while. Take the phone book, for

[2]

[3]

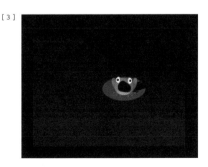

17

example: You name your child Richard Head, you wait twenty years, you get a laugh. Or think of the largest block of consumer-created content in the world: classified advertising. Even your grandmother put in a classified. She crafted something, and it was published. Some of the changes that have made consumer-created content such a big trend today include the reduction in the cost of distribution and the reduction in the cost of authorship tools. Everyone has access to this stuff all of a sudden, and as a result you have people making music, people blogging, people creating videos or spending Sunday afternoons rating and reviewing books for free. There are online communities about the weirdest things, like knitting stuffed animals. And of course, there's this explosion recently in online photography and online video. I tried my hand at some of these participatory projects, which I called "Toilet Paper Fashion"[4] or "When Office Supplies Attack,"[5] where people sent me pictures of themselves dressed in toilet paper or being attacked by paper clips and other office supplies.

But even for these projects I was still generating rule sets, I was still doing a lot of the work. So in 2002, I came out with a really crappy online version of Photoshop that allows people to make and submit their own drawings for an online gallery on my site.

[4]

toilet paper fashion

[5]

when office supplies attack

About twenty thousand images have come in now, which is pretty cool, but this kind of application rewards people who are good at drawing. People who are bad at drawing send me pictures of penises, and that isn't really the kind of site I want to run, overall. My first attempt to change that was to create a program called "The Scribbler," which actually tried to reward people for bad drawing. You draw your crappy illustration here, and the Scribbler converts it to a postwar German etching over time. All these examples were submitted by kids under the age of fifteen. But I still got penises. My second attempt was more passive-aggressive: In this version anything you draw morphs into the shape of a penis.[6]

I wasn't just making penis jokes for the hell of it, though. It was a kind of larger metaphor. The problem with inviting the audience to participate is that people will do things that you're not asking them to do. They veer off in other directions. So there are two focuses to this crap-o-copia. One is usually used in the negative when people comment that there's so much more **crap** being made. It's just daunting to sift through this large, large supply of consumer-created content. But of course, there's another way to look at it, which is that there's so much more crap **being made**. Never before in the history of man have more people been involved in creating and

---

[6]

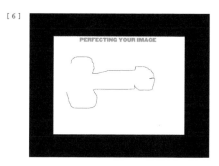

in substantiating opinions outside of themselves. And this became really interesting to me. I started to think about the audience as a population that's learning a new language, but it happens to be **our** language. They're learning the language of production. The fact that the audience now has favorite fonts is weird! That's how we used to tell each other apart. "Are you a designer yet? Prove it." "Helvetica." "Oh, absolutely." But now these terms have become commonplace.

Today we're talking about "Designing Audiences." What I love about this title is the proximity encoded in it: it feels like it's missing something—a preposition of some kind—and there is this sort of neckercube effect: the meaning changes depending on whether you understand "designing" as a transitive verb affecting "audience" or as an intransitive verb. Is it "Designing Audiences," a how-to guide for graphic designers, or is it really about an audience of designers? What's interesting about this neckercube effect is that you can't really conceive of both at the same time.

Usually, the topic of the audience being empowered in this kind of way is seen as a situation where on the one side you have this ivory tower of designers sitting there with their really large watches, naming their children after font families of Emigre and giving each other awards so they don't have to deal with that most vulgar of all categories: "Most Popular." Meanwhile, on the other side is a mass, the large audience of people wearing iron-on T-shirts that say, "I'm with Stupid," mixing Remy Martin with Coca-Cola, and carrying around Polaroids of kittens just in case something's customizable. Of course, it's easy to view things in such a black-and-white way. We tend to do that with all these emergent technologies: Is photography going to destroy painting for good? Is the printing press going to destroy the church? But instead

of doing that, I think it's far more helpful to look at the topic from the perspective that the audience brings with it a lot of valuable additions. They bring opinion, they bring information, attitude, perspective. There are some designers who have made a conscious choice to involve the audience in the process of their projects. Tonight we're going to meet some of them and talk about different aspects of dealing with the audience, working with the audience, and learning from the audience.
So here we have Stefan Bucher, Katie Salen, and Eric Rodenbeck.

Applause

Enter
Stefan G. Bucher,
Katie Salen,
Eric Rodenbeck

Stefan created the sites 344design.com, store344.com, and dailymonster.com. He's the author and designer of <u>All Access: The Making of Thirty Extraordinary Graphic Designers</u> (2006). He has done work for David Hockney, Tarsem, and the general manager of Per Se, and creates an illustrated column, "Ink and Circumstance," for <u>STEP Inside Design</u> magazine. On November 9, 2006, he filmed himself blowing some ink on a piece of paper and making it into a monster drawing. He linked the result to his blog, and for the next ninety-nine days, he posted a new monster every night. And that is how his popular site, dailymonster.com, came to be.

Next, we have Katie Salen. As a game designer, writer, and design educator, Katie has worked on a range of projects for clients such as Microsoft, SIGGRAPH, the Hewlett Foundation, XMedia Lab, the Design Institute, Gamelab, and mememe productions. She coauthored <u>Rules of Play: Game Design Fundamentals</u> (2003) and <u>The Game Design Reader: A Rules of Play Anthology</u> (2005), both from MIT Press, and she's currently working on several MacArthur Foundation-funded projects that focus on digital media and learning. She was a contributing writer for <u>Res</u> magazine and worked as an animator on Richard Linklater's animated feature <u>Waking Life</u>. With collaborators Marina Zurkow and Nancy Nowacek she recently completed Karaoke Ice, a project featuring an ice cream truck outfitted for traveling karaoke.

And last, we have Eric Rodenbeck. Eric Rodenbeck is the founder and creative director of Stamen Design, where his projects have focused on exploring the limits of online media and live information visualization. Eric and his team work with a diverse range of clients, including MoveOn.org, Digg, Yahoo, BMW, Adobe, and the San Francisco Museum of Modern Art. Prior to founding Stamen, Eric led the data-driven

[7] From left to right: Ze Frank, Stefan G. Bucher, Katie Salen, Eric Rodenbeck

narrative effort at Quokka Sports. He also illustrated and designed for <u>Wired</u> magazine and Wired Books and was a cofounder of the design collective Umwow. He has lectured and spoken at Yale University and South by Southwest, among others.

First, Stefan is going to tell us a little bit about his work.

Music video   STEFAN G. BUCHER: Since we only have a little bit of time, I put together a quick video of my work for you.

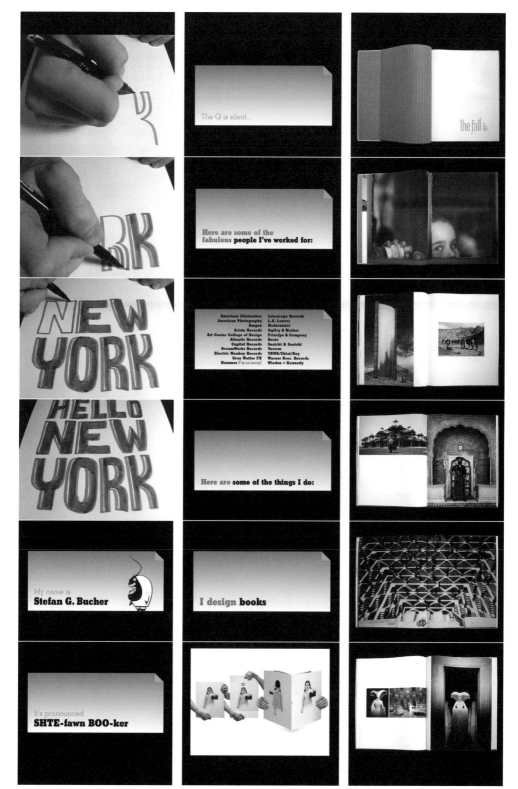

BUCHER: As you can see, I started out as a print whore. I got into the whole online designing audiences thing only recently and more or less by mistake. I started drawing monsters because an image appeared to me one day—in a sort of nonalcoholic, nonscary way—of a monster crawling up my arm. I spun that initial image into a series of drawings that turned into a book called Upstairs Neighbors. While I was waiting for old-world publishers to come to a decision about the book, I decided to film myself drawing some new monsters and put the videos online on my then brand-new blog. I thought that maybe ten or twenty of my friends would take a look at it.

But the link to my site very quickly got forwarded and all of a sudden I had a similar experience to Ze's: My web traffic increased as all these people were coming to see the drawings. So I invited them to name the monsters, but instead of just naming them, people actually made up stories about them—really good, cool, long ones. I would post a new video clip at midnight, and by 2 a.m. the first stories would appear. It was just amazing. In order to foster this kind of involvement I included a speech bubble at the end of each clip that says, "What's the story?" to let people know that I want them to participate. I wrote the text upside down, just to show off. A lot of people actually responded very well to that.

But wait...

There's more!

I did one hundred of the monster clips. Because I do everything in a multiple of 344, I initially thought, "Oh, I'll do 344 monsters," but I quickly figured out that my head would explode. So I capped it at one hundred. As we got close to Daily Monster 100, one of the visitors to the site, Charlotte Saylor, suggested that I put an inkblot up on the website so that people could make monsters on their own. That was the beginning of the Open Source Monsters. The inkblots can be downloaded as pdf files and printed out in order to make your own drawings.

[12] OPEN SOURCE MONSTERS, by Andy Wick, Heather Sebastian, Adam Duquette, Corwin Parker, Stefan G. Bucher
[13] DAILY MONSTER QUILT, by Annie Nordmark

Original Ink Blot

Andy Wick

Heather Sebastian

Adam Duquette

Corwin Parker

Me, too!

I was completely stunned by all the energy and the goodwill that people brought to the site. They were obviously supereager to contribute and to make their own things. The site started out as a way for me to pass the time and to promote my book, but it very quickly grew into this great online community. One person sent me a photo of a monster quilt she made. She picked thirteen of her favorite monsters and made a huge monster quilt. She actually told me that the photo's somewhat blurry because she and her husband got a bit frisky on the quilt when they took the picture. So while Ze gets penis drawings, I just get people telling me that they got frisky.

Laughs

[14] THE DAILY MONSTER, selected frames from the video series by Stefan G. Bucher

On another part of the site I asked people to contribute segments to the World's Tallest Monster. I drew the head and the feet and had other people send in segments to make up the rest of the monster. Originally, I thought, "That's going to take off. That's going to be huge." But it actually became a niche thing. I'm finding that everybody responds to different parts of the site. Some people really like writing stories but they don't like to draw, other people like to draw on the inkblots, and others again just like to make these little segments for the World's Tallest Monster.

[15] THE WORLD'S TALLEST MONSTER, selected segments by various contributors from the ongoing project at tallestmonster.com

By now the monsters have found their way into almost everything I do. A cover I did for the UCLA Extension catalog has six monsters hidden in it and they are the focus of an illustration that appeared in New York magazine a couple of weeks ago. I'm also selling some of the monster drawings. They are so much fun to do that I thought, "Maybe there's a way I can make a living off of it." A friend invited me to submit my drawing to a gallery, so these monsters are for sale at Art For Empty Walls.

A couple of days ago I launched my own online store—called Store344, of course. I'm going to start making products in the same way that I did the monsters, producing things that I would like to have for myself, but also listening to what people are requesting. "I really want to have monster buttons," somebody emailed me this week, so I'm going to make those.

[16] UCLA Extension Catalog (Fall 2007), by Stefan G. Bucher, curated by InJu Sturgeon

[17] HIGH PRIORITY illustration for New York magazine, by Stefan G. Bucher, commissioned by Rob Hewitt

UCLA Extension *of quarter begins September 22, 2007*

THE WEEK

Lastly, because I am a print whore, I do have two monster books coming out next year. One is the original <u>Upstairs Neighbors</u>, which is what started it all. The other is a book and DVD about the website with all the collected stories, called <u>100 Days of Monsters</u>. A lot of the stories are really funny. Somebody saw this monster [19] and immediately said, "Oh, you know, this guy had a zucchini-related emergency." A frequent contributor by the name of Bill Bibo wrote a great parody of a commercial for Jack Coosteau's Tadpole City, which has everything to fill your tadpole needs.

[18] *UPSTAIRS NEIGHBORS*, cover of the forthcoming book by Stefan G. Bucher
[19] *100 DAYS OF MONSTERS*, spread from the forthcoming book by Stefan G. Bucher

[18]

[19]

Before I leave the stage for Katie, I want to show you one more monster, one of my recent favorites. In the animation of this monster it turns out that his little rat tail works like a bicycle pump. It pumps up his mullet and then he floats away.

And that's all I have. Thank you very much.

KATIE SALEN: Hello. I'm a game designer, so one thing that makes me a little bit different than Eric and Stefan is that my work **requires** an audience; without an audience, a game doesn't really live. My work is inherently interactive, and I've become very interested in something I call the "magic circle." When you create something, you can think about that work existing within the space of a circle. The meaning of the work resides in that space, and when you publish it, you invite people in to negotiate those meanings with you. The "ordinary" world, in some sense, exists outside of that circle. I think the traditional view of designer and audience is that there's a boundary separating them. In game design, what begins to happen is that that threshold, that boundary, becomes a space of invitation. Recently, I've been spending a lot of time thinking about how to design permission slips that allow an audience to enter into the work. I think that question is at the core of what we're talking about today. Participation is not something that happens for no apparent reason. There're specific conditions that allow people to enter into the things we create. Stefan, you talked about the fact that some people responded more to certain kinds of rules than others. Ze, I'm sure you found that, too, in some of your work. I'm trying to understand what those conditions are that allow people to feel that they're invited to participate in the work, either as its producers or as audience members.

[21] KARAOKE ICE (2006) is a project by Nancy Nowacek, Katie Salen, and Marina Zurkow. Tinklepop produced and arranged by Lem Jay Ignacio. Produced in collaboration with students and graduates of the San Jose State Cadre Laboratory for New Media. Shown here: "disco ball."

About a year ago, two friends (Marina Zurkow and Nancy Nowacek) and I received a commission to produce a piece of public art for the ISEA/ZeroOne festival in San José, California. The theme was "the interactive city." We started to think about forms that were participatory in urban culture, and we hit on karaoke. None of us were karaoke buffs, but we felt it was a framework that gave people permission to get up on stage and, in some sense, act ridiculous. There's something so empowering and open about the system that we wanted to look at it more closely. We were also deeply interested in the concept of character-as-interface. We realized that characters—like the truck and squirrel cub we ended up designing—make better interfaces for interaction than traditional computer interfaces where you just press a button.

We asked ourselves, "How can we combine the notion of karaoke as a participatory medium and the notion of character-as-interface?" And we came up with a project called Karaoke Ice, which consisted of an ice cream truck that was turned into a mobile karaoke stage, driven by a mute squirrel, who functioned as the emcee. The squirrel was part of this notion of character-as-interface and became the permission slip that allowed people to enter into this weird space. We made a short video to give you a better idea of the project.

Music video

[22] KARAOKE ICE (2006), truck before its transformation
[23] REMEDIOS THE SQUIRREL CUB, costume design

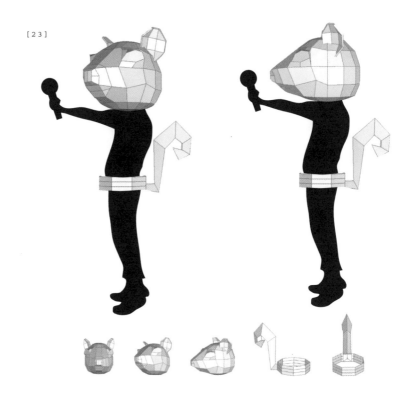

[24] MONTAGE of music video featuring Karaoke Ice

47

It was our big fear that people wouldn't participate, that they wouldn't karaoke, but they were actually lining up. Karaoke Ice is, in some ways, the most interactive work I have ever been a part of designing. It was incredible to see how people felt so comfortable stepping inside this crazy fiction of the squirrel. Besides using a character as the interface for the experience, we also drew the audience in by playing on the idea of a gift economy. The truck gave you free icies and you gave her a song. Even though the truck gave something to the audience for free, there was an innate expectation that people had to give something back. I'm really interested in the notion of the gift as something that actually requires something of the recipient. Nancy, Marina, and I saw that in this particular project people indeed felt compelled to reciprocate.

[25] KARAOKE ICE (2006), Marina and Katie get their karaoke on.

So we had the character—the truck and the squirrel—we had the audience, and then, of course, we had the performer. The truck travels from city to city and has a customized song list specific to each location. There are only twenty-one songs available per city, and only seven per day. We wanted to limit the choices people had, hoping that the expression that came out of those limited choices would have greater value. We were looking at karaoke as a folk database, consisting of a set of songs that people of a specific area and culture sing and re-sing over and over again. A sense of identity and the character of a place merge in the uniqueness of these performances. So this project really values the performer as the content. The karaoke truck itself is simply a framework to give people the opportunity to speak.

Applause   FRANK: Thank you.

Hey Ya

Material Girl

Heart of Glass

Creep

Work It

I Want You To Want Me

The Harder They Come

Superstition

You Shook Me All Night Long

Hurt

Hotel California

Blister in the Sun

Respect

Lucy in the Sky With Diamonds

Ring of Fire

Killing Me Softly

I Want to Be Sedated

It's the End of the World as We Know It

Kiss

These Boots Are Made for Walking

You Really Got Me

ERIC RODENBECK: Hello. I'm here from Stamen in San Francisco. We are a team of six designer-technology people, with none of us formally trained in what we do. These days our studio is mostly involved in mapping-related work, both geographical and nongeographical. We're calling this mapping of different kinds of information spaces "data visualization." Just about all of our work takes place on the Internet, although we're exploring books and other physical media as places where data visualization can happen.

What I want to talk about a little today—and we'll find some intersections between the theme of designing audiences and this—is the notion that data visualization is a medium. In our age there's all this information floating around on the Internet, and it's increasingly easy to measure things, it's increasingly easy to track things over time. It's starting to get past the point where you can deal with it all by looking at lists and static charts. As more and more of the world moves online, and more and more data moves online, there need to be other ways of representing that kind of information. At Stamen we think that data visualization is not really a technology or a methodology, but a medium that we can work in—a medium like print or film. I want to give you some examples of the potential of this medium and how it can not only be useful but address a wide range of expressive concerns.

[27] GRAFFITI ARCHAEOLOGY, by Cassidy Curtis and Stamen (Eric Rodenbeck). Cassidy Curtis's Graffiti Archaeology project is a collage of photos of San Francisco graffiti taken from 1998 to the present. Stamen built the framework that lets viewers explore the space of this visual urban landscape over time.

Current Layer: 11 november 2006. Photos by Jake Dobkin

The following project was done by Michael Gastner, Cosma Shalizi, and Mark Newman at the University of Michigan in 2004. This [28] is a map of the results of the last election, showing the red states and the blue states. Because of the electoral college system, if a party wins a state, it gets all of the votes in that state. So this is the map that you would have seen on Fox News and a bunch of other places.

If you take a closer look at the electoral results, though, and break them down by county and not just by state, you get a different kind of map, on which the red and the blue start to look a little bit more mottled and a little bit less monolithic. [29] And if you take those results and color-code each one of those counties by the degree to which it's red or blue, you get an even more subtle picture. You start to see urban archipelagos; you see lots and lots of not quite red, not quite blue places, as well as some red and blue strongholds. [30]

Then, if you take this more subtle map and adjust the size of the counties according to their population, you get something that looks like this. [31] It's a cartogram. I'm not sure this is the most easily understood map of the country, but it is certainly a more provocative way of looking at the data. The United States, which in the first map was represented as a sea of red with a few little blue places floating on its edges, turns out to be much more variegated, much more interspersed, and much, much denser. Today these kinds of visualizations are starting to become more accessible to the public. People are getting much more comfortable with maps, and there's an increasing literacy forming around these visualizations.

[28-31] MAPS visualizing the results of the 2004 presidential election based on increasingly detailed data sets, by Michael Gastner, Cosma Shalizi, Mark Newman, University of Michigan, 2004

[28]

[29]

[30]

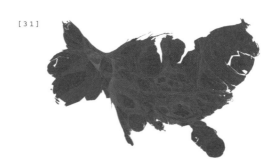

[31]

One of my favorite blogs is indexed.blogspot.com, where Jessica Hagy puts up a new chart every couple of days. I thought this [32] one was just awesome. A is striptease, B is limbo, C is polka, and D is dances involving poles. Jessica is playing with the notion that charts and graphs are their own language and can be manipulated. Charts and graphs can have a lot of expressive potential and make us look at things differently.

Percentage of Chart Which Resembles Pac-man is also one of my big favorites. [33] (Unfortunately, I haven't been able to find out who the author is.) The basic point for us is that data visualization is a medium like film or video or pottery. It's something that can be used to entertain or to inform, as well as to describe or analyze or illustrate. It's a medium that can be used for a wide range of purposes. The subset of this medium that Stamen has been working in is mostly live data. The kinds of data that are becoming more and more available are often those that get updated regularly, sometimes every few seconds. Live data has some interesting problems associated with it—primarily that you never know just what kinds of results you're going to get, so it's tough to design frameworks that always work. But the exciting thing about this way of working is that you're always being surprised by what comes up on the screen.

[32] CHART OF DANCES INVOLVING POLES by Jessica Hagy, http://indexed.blogspot.com

[33] PERCENTAGE OF CHART WHICH RESEMBLES PACMAN, author unknown

[3 2]

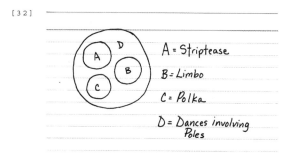

A = Striptease

B = Limbo

C = Polka

D = Dances involving Poles

[3 3]

Percentage of Chart Which Resembles Pac–man

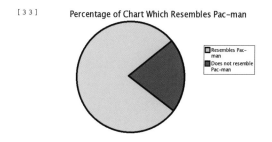

Resembles Pac–man

Does not resemble Pac–man

For the last year or so Stamen's been working with digg.com, a social news site that lets people vote on whether they think a story is interesting or not. It sounds pretty simple, but over a million people have signed up for the site and are "Digging" many thousands of stories each day. People follow each others' stories and recommend them to one another, so there's quite a complex ecosystem of data there, which is highly interconnected and a great indication of what an Internet population cares about *right now.* It's gotten so popular and moves so quickly that standard list-based ways of dealing with stories and voting aren't as effective as they could be, so Stamen creates visualizations of this data that give people a richer and deeper view of what's happening on the site at any given time. Our "maps" are live tools that pull data from the constantly changing landscape of what people are doing on Digg and represent them in a rich and interactive graphic language.

[34-35] Visualizations of live data from digg.com, accessible at labs.digg.com. Since early 2006, Stamen has been collaborating with Digg on visualization projects.

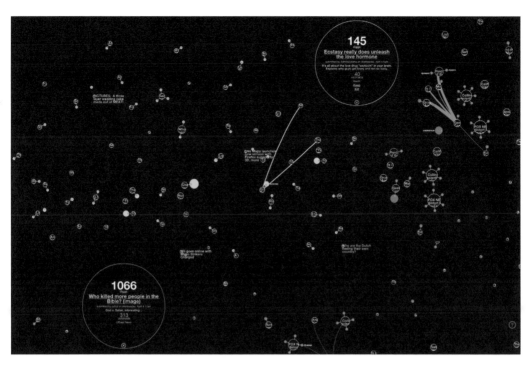

Another project that we just worked on with Trulia,
a real estate aggregation site, is a map visualizing
home sales in the United States, animated over time.
Our first map was of San Francisco, and you can see
the city starting out as a few tiny little dots on a couple
of different hills, and then after the 1906 earthquake
there is this incredible explosion of growth flowing
over and around and under the different geographic
features of the city. It looks almost like a virus—people
are just taking over. It's kind of scary, watching the way
we're spreading out over the whole country, but it's also
quite interesting to understand the ebbs and flows that
humans operate inside of over long periods of time.
You can also do searches and key in your address, and
it's a joy to explore these enormous records of urban
development. On the Los Angeles map, for example,
you can really see the housing boom happening. The
maps show that different cities and neighborhoods have
different kinds of growth. Some of them are organic,

Applause
some of them are not.

[36-38] TRULIA HINDSIGHT is an animated view onto the Trulia real
estate database, with an eye toward exposing patterns of expansion
and development through home construction dates. Shown here: growth
patterns in San Francisco.

FRANK: Thank you. Now we're going to talk about some of the broader themes. Obviously, not every project out there is suitable for inviting users to come in. The work we've seen so far includes some very different types of projects with very different kinds of audiences. The first thing that I'd like to talk about is the loss of control that is involved in handing the reins over to the audience. There are really two questions here: One is, how do you exert control over your audiences; the other is, in what circumstances do you cede control to your audiences, and how does it make you feel?

Stefan, why don't we start with you?

BUCHER: Well, I'm not exactly a control freak, but certainly a control enthusiast.

FRANK: I don't believe you at all. Before this show, you spent about ten minutes trying to adjust the gamma settings on the projector so your video looked right on the screen, which is, I think, the beginning of a problem, because everyone at home is looking at your website on monitors that they haven't calibrated.

BUCHER: So I'm a control aficionado. In print design—and I have gone over this with my shrink—you can find a tiny slice of the universe that you can control completely. The H is away from the E by just **this** much. So it is a bit scary to create something, to put it out there, and to have other people screwing around with it. But I got over it really quickly, because it became so much fun. Of course, I didn't set out to do it, and I think if somebody had said, "I want you to do something that surrenders control," I probably would have said, "Oh, I don't want to do that." Originally, I thought of my website as an online gallery, but then the audience just took over. When I realized that,

Laughs

Laughs

[39] DAILYMONSTER.COM, website homepage

Stefan G. Bucher's DAILY MONSTER:

http://dailymonster.com/

WELCOME TO
STEFAN G. BUCHER'S
DAILY MONSTER
DRAWINGS, STORIES, THINGS: SHOW ME YOUR MONSTERS & I'LL SHOW YOU MINE.

February 25, 2007

DAILY MONSTER 100 (of 100)

Good morning. Thank you for being here for the big finale—*Number 100*—The last of the Daily Monsters. But before we get to that, let me direct you towards yesterday's amazing stories. Everybody's just kicking ass on these last few creatures. It's such a pleasure to see such great posts from all of you—new contributors, monster stalwarts, and returning champions alike. Please take some time to read the entries. They're worth your time:

CATEGORIES

344 WORK **DAILY MONSTER** ILLUSTRATION LIFE NEW WORK OPEN SOURCE MONSTERS STORE 344 TALLEST MONSTER TECH GEEKINESS WEEKLY MONSTER

STORE 344

STORE 344

Buy Daily Monster prints and originals and lots of 344 goodies at the brand new STORE 344

DAILY MONSTER 001

START FROM THE BEGINNING

DAILY MONSTER 100

START FROM THE END

WORLD'S TALLEST MONSTER

Help the World's Tallest Monster grow! Click here and add your section today!

RECENT POSTS

WEEKLY MONSTER 100

I immediately thought, "How can I control them? How can I now hack the audience to actually participate more?"

FRANK: So in what ways did you do that?

BUCHER: The first thing for me was to realize that people wanted to post stories, and then to make it as easy for them as possible. Initially, I just put up a little banner that said, "Post your story here," but some of the people who were drawn to my illustrations weren't used to navigating blogs and didn't know how to post their comments. So I explained that and I also made sure to go online and praise all the individual stories every night.

FRANK: Oh, my lord. You praised all the individual stories? But I have to ask you: There was no failure whatsoever in the presentation that you just showed, so did you just have a remarkably wonderful, efficient audience that submitted perfect stuff every time? Or were you exerting some control there?

BUCHER: No, I think I got lucky. There wasn't anything I had to take off, no one was screwing around, or putting up epithets, or anything like that. It was kind of a perfect birth. The great moment for me was when visitors to my site started talking to each other. In the beginning people were just talking to me, writing things like, "I made this story for you, what do you think?" But then they started commenting on each other's stories. For example, a guy called Terry T. contributed a story every day, and people would come online and write, "Oh, Terry, what a cool story, I can't wait for tomorrow." So it became a stand-alone thing.

SALEN: Did the participants get upset when other people tried to give them ideas about where their story

Here you see the inimitable norf, in its home habitat of the sea of Mars. Scientists currently think that the sea is frozen, but they will soon find that it only appears to be frozen; it is actually a frothy mix of salt water, nitrogen and Dippin' Dots. In this nurturing environment, the inimitable norf raises her young, soaring through the slightly viscous mixture and keeping a close eye on her calf.

By Catherine Matthew | February 09, 2007 at 07:26am

Emlyn, age 4, says: These monsters are happy, sad and mad. They're going to Texas. They will live there. They will live outside. They will play with lots and lots and lots of toys. Their names are "Scary" and "Little."

By Sarah Schopp | February 09, 2007 at 11:18am

Englebrectt was born a large baby and never stopped growing. By the time he was three he was ten times the size of his father, who had to float around him to keep him in line. Englebrectt was a smart kid and became the protector of his village in the lawn. Whenever one hears a chunk in the lawn mower, that is Englebrectt, putting a kibosh on the chopping of the blades of grass.

By Thibaut Paciello | February 09, 2007 at 06:23pm

The two swam with each other for the majority of the day. The smaller one was ready for her next step in life. The small growth spurt would be the first of many, but luckily, they weren't painful in any way. Mostly, the growing seasons saw several younglings very active and excited. The mothers would have quite the handful keeping up with their offspring's heightened energy levels. Ultimately, the biggest problem facing the parents of these little tykes (and by little, it must be said that they were the size of a small aircraft carrier) was their enormous appetites. Feeding these little guys was always an incredible undertaking. Good thing there are a lot of tasty meat sticks atop floating chunks of metal on the water's surface.

By Terry Tolleson | February 09, 2007 at 09:16pm

should go? Did the notion of exerting control affect the participants as well, or were they very open?

BUCHER: They were really, really open. I never had an instance where somebody said, "Oh, that's a stupid story, that monster isn't about that at all; it's about this." It was almost creepy in a kumbaya kind of way how everybody got along and everybody was incredibly supportive. Most people just said, "Wow, I love this story, here's mine." Once somebody wrote, "God, your story's so good that I didn't want to post mine." That's why I went in and made sure to leave comments about everyone's stories as much as I could to let them know that every story is appreciated.

Laughs

FRANK: That's interesting—the notion of something being so good that you're afraid to participate. I would imagine that can be a real killer in a project like Karaoke Ice. Is that, to some extent, the reason why you chose ice cream truck music?

SALEN: Partly. Earlier you mentioned the fact that while you want people to contribute, you still want to maintain some sense of quality control. Sometimes we don't love it when participants make what we might consider to be crap. A lot of tools that are developed for users include a built-in modicum of quality to allow them to produce stuff that allows them to feel good about what they're producing, that allows them to operate a little bit on a level playing field. Of course, there will always be experts within that system. But the trick is to design the system in such a way that both novices and masters can coexist and learn from each other.

FRANK: And how does one do that? Is it a matter of setting boundary conditions, or constraints, that make the people who are just going to make crap go away because they don't want to put in the five minutes required to fulfill these conditions?

SALEN: In the field of game design, we talk about designing rule sets—which basically means designing constraints, or boundary conditions, that limit what a player can do and cannot do. You create a framework for people to act within, a framework with certain kinds of qualities. For example, many drawing tools constrain how you can draw in very particular ways, based on the kinds of marks those tools allow you to make. In a lot of games, doing level design doesn't mean you design from scratch, without limitations on the palette you have to work with. You're given pieces and constraints to design with. In this way there's some sense of evenness in the work produced, and people learn how to become quite masterful working within such constrained contexts.

FRANK: Eric, in your work, I get the feeling that people often don't know that they're subjects of a project, at least in its beginning stages.

RODENBECK: Right.

FRANK: In a recent interview for the podcast CreativeXpert you said that your experience in architecture school made you a little wary of top-down control, and that you were more interested in the idea of studying and playing with emergent content coming up from the audience. In some way that probably has boundaries in the spectrum of control and non-control as well.

RODENBECK: For sure. I think that I'm more of a gardener than an architect. I much prefer to plant something and see how it grows than to imagine it all in my head or plan it out on paper. I think that's why we work with live data flows. The world itself is so much more interesting than any logo I could come up with or any color choice that I might make. There's this flow of information that's happening all around us, whether it's people voting on something, people putting photos of their lives on the Internet to share, or taxicabs moving around San Francisco; all these things are measurable. There's an organic quality that comes from that, of people actually doing things, instead of me deciding what they should do. What I find most interesting about this kind of live data is negotiating that flow and pulling out the different emphases and de-emphases.

FRANK: What I find so interesting about bringing the audience into one's work is that there is a stock and standard set of tools already out there, for example voting mechanisms, comments, or message boards. A lot of your work begins at those places and then starts tweaking outward from those platforms that are supplying information in a particular way. I think to some extent all those tools are like rule sets that are driving the activity in a particular direction.

RODENBECK: Well, I don't know how well known it is, but Flickr, which is kind of the golden child of a social network based on user-generated content, originally came out of a sprawling, rule-based online game system. The game, developed by Caterina Fake, Stewart Butterfield, and Ben Cerveny, was called Game Never Ending. It was a virtual space where you could walk around and do all

[43-45] CABSPOTTING, by Eric Rodenbeck, Mike Migurski, Shawn Allen, and Tomas Apodaca, consists of visualizations of GPS data generated by Yellow Cab taxicabs in San Francisco.

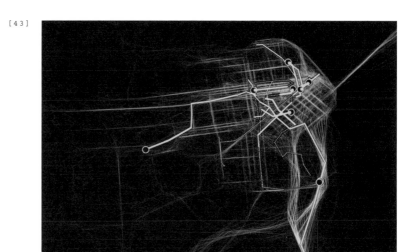

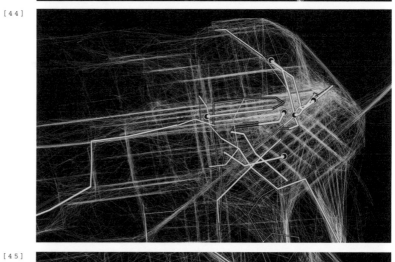

kinds of complex activities. For example, if you picked up enough sheets of paper and a printing press, you could open up a book company and disseminate your ideas that way. As you got further along in the game, you could determine your own rule sets. It was this crazy, abstract notion of a game never ending. And eventually…

FRANK: Nobody wanted to play it, they just wanted to share photographs.

RODENBECK: Nobody wanted to play it, it was too much like the online version of the Sims game, where instead of playing against the computer and the game itself (as you do in the local version), all you're doing is interact with other people through the Sims framework, getting them to like you and be your friend, etc. It turns out that it's really boring; no one wants to do it, because you can do that in real life. In the end Caterina and Stewart basically ran out of money and decided that they needed to come up with something that was going to pay the rent. So they decided to build a site that used a lot of the same rules they had been developing for Game Never Ending, but to make it all about uploading pictures. So from there, Flickr started and became one of the best interactive social networks around. At least that's one story. I love the accidental quality of that, but I also love that Flickr developed from gaming rules. Game Never Ending never really took off, but it was the crucial groundwork that was needed to create Flickr. I think that's something that is becoming more and more important, that rules which are already very well established in computer games are starting to move their way online. It's not just a big, crazy free-for-all anymore. There are mechanisms and levers, there's a language and a literacy that people are starting to develop.

[46-47] BACKCHANNEL is another of Stamen's visualization projects. These charts show a real-time view of the conversation happening in the #etech IRC channel at O'Reilly's Emerging Technology Conference.

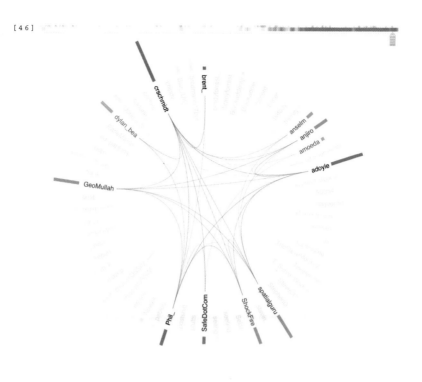

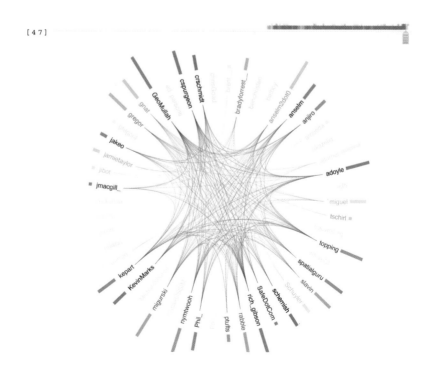

FRANK: In each of your cases, the idea of feedback, in other words, watching something grow and then latching onto "interesting results" is essential. It strikes me that one part of exerting control is just not paying attention to some of the results while playing off of others.
If everyone started posting cat pictures on your bulletin board, you wouldn't necessarily rename your enterprise "pictures of cats." So how does one choose?

Laughs

SALEN: That's a complicated question.

Laughs

FRANK: Yes, you've got two minutes.

SALEN: I think there's a tipping point. Part of it has to do with what your vision is for the project and where you want it to go. In interactive work, you're always testing what you create with the people that are using it, even in the early stages of a project. Often they don't respond to what you think they should be responding to, but instead they discover all of these interesting other things you hadn't really thought about. You have a choice at that point to embrace what the audience thought was interesting and make that your own, or to say, "Okay, that's interesting, but I want people to really understand this other thing," and then find a way to design them back toward your particular path.
I think there's something interesting happening now: there is a sense of ownership developing within participatory culture, a point at which the users or the audience make claim to the system as their own, and the designer cedes control with that. Often this phenomenon is temporary; they take it over and then they give it back. I think of it as a negotiation between the original creator and the people that are using his creation—a kind of emergent call-and-response structure. We can't think of

[48] KARAOKE ICE (2006), fan art

the things we build anymore as stable objects. They're not stable at all; they are subject to ebbs and flows. As a designer you just have to choose how you're going to work within those ebbs and flows and when you choose to try and push the audience back. So while you do have a vision for your site or game or project, you listen, I think, as well.

FRANK: I'm just going to dovetail this into the next question, which is about scale. In some projects that involve audiences, you might only have twenty people at your disposal, while in another scenario you might have hundreds of thousands, if not millions. How does scale affect your thinking about a project? Stefan, would the specialness of your site last if you had two hundred thousand people a day drawing monsters?

BUCHER: I think scale can change the vibe a little bit. A while ago I was posted on a Brazilian porn site. It was literally boobs, boobs, boobs, **monsters**, boobs, boobs, boobs. And the nature of the comments I received changed for a couple of days. They were much more of the sort, "Hey, cool, love it. I'm going back to the boobs now." Obviously, at that point my interaction with the people that post is different. I'm not getting into some sort of big correspondence with them. With an increasing amount of people visiting the site, it becomes less personal. When it's a smaller group you can nurture it a bit more and be more personally involved with the individual people that make up the group.

FRANK: Eric, have you done any small-scale projects?

Laughs

RODENBECK: No, I don't get out of bed for less than $10,000. Do you mean small-scale in the sense that only a couple of people are paying attention to it?

[49]

FRANK: No, actually the other way around, but you can answer it how you want.

RODENBECK: The important thing in the visualization projects—just to segue from the user-generated content for a moment—is not so much that there's a huge amount of data, but rather that the data is going to come reliably, that there's a consistent data feed, that there's something that can be measured. A good example of this is Dopplr, Matt Biddulph's new project. Dopplr.com is a site for travelers that tracks where you and your friends are going to be in the world; you enter your trips, your friends enter their trips, and the site lets you see where you and your friends overlap. There are about nine hundred people on it or something like that, and it's a very different situation from a network like Digg or Flickr where thousands of interactions are happening every minute, so the visualization challenges are of a whole different type. We've done some visualization based on the data collected on the site so you can see everybody on Dopplr who's going to be in Barcelona in May, and even though the data's not live or huge, it's fairly consistent and it just keeps on coming. So for us it's not so much an issue of whether the data set is big enough, it's more important that it is going to continue. Generally, I think, if something is good, people are going to use it, they're going to talk about it, to spread the word, and it's going to grow. Ze, you experienced this with your invitation. You did something for thirteen people and then it ballooned. If it's good, people will find it. I think that's true.

FRANK: Wow, that's a big statement—if it's good, it will balloon. I mean, CNN has a most popular news stories of the day, and it invariably is an animal trapped in something.

Laughs

[50-51] 16THANDMISSION, by Eric Rodenbeck and Alon Salant, is another project that was built on reliable, if infrequent, data, in this case from nextbus.com. The project visualizes an urban environment (the corner of 16th and Mission streets) by bringing harvested live bus schedule data into representations of the space itself.

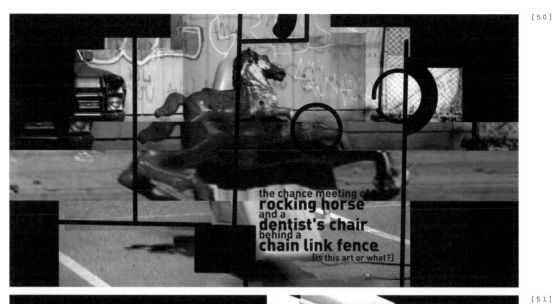

the chance meeting of a
rocking horse
and a
dentist's chair
behind a
chain link fence
[is this art or what?]

RODENBECK: Sure. Bruce Sterling is fond of ripping apart the assertion that out of ten million blogs, some of them just have to be good. He says that that's like saying, if you throw enough toasters into the air, one of them just has to be able to fly. But I don't think I'm saying that. I'm saying if you put something up that actually **is** good, then people are going to use it, and it's going to get more successful.

FRANK: I think it is often remarkable when something you put online results in lots of energy, even though people are making stuff that looks like crap. They're still doing it and they love doing it. So with some of these projects across the spectrum, you can't really look at the outcome, the product, as the success of the project. Have you been in situations like that, where you're amazed at what's happening, but you feel that you can't really show the results to anyone necessarily?

Laughs

BUCHER: I think the karaoke truck is sort of the singing equivalent to some of the drawings people send me. They're not necessarily the most technically accomplished illustrations or songs, but if you give them the proper framework, just the fact that the site is breathing makes it cool and makes it interesting. What I'm trying to figure out is how to develop the best gallery setting so that the drawings I get from five-year-olds still look good when I put them next to some of the more accomplished ones. People need to understand where the various pieces are coming from and be able to feel the underlying positive, creative energy. The challenge is to present the work in a way that makes everybody look pretty good. But so far, I haven't received a drawing where I thought, "Oh, I can't possibly show this because it's just too awful."

[52] OPEN SOURCE MONSTER 10, by Sam Berkes

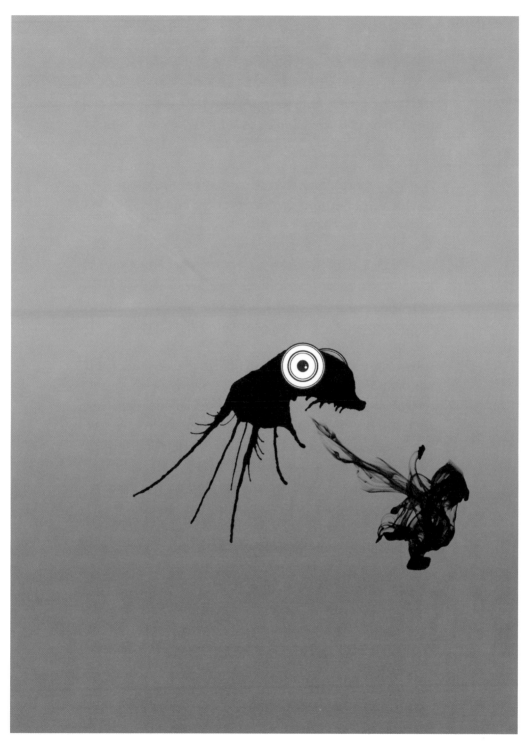

SALEN: I also think it's not just about showing the final piece on its own; it's part of this larger circuit of production. There is a beginning point, there are people that are participating, there's feedback being given. The challenge now is how to represent this work as a whole, and I think you have to represent it differently than we have in the past.

FRANK: So there's an idiom of consumer-created or consumer-generated content that we need to rely on to appreciate this work?

SALEN: Well, with Karaoke Ice, for instance, the original idea was to record people as they performed and then play the recordings as the truck drove around different neighborhoods. What we realized is that people sound terrible.

Laughs

When you take the recording—this artifact—out of the moment of the performance, it is completely changed and begins to have a different set of values attached to it. We decided that we couldn't decontextualize the performance in that way. We eventually uploaded the clips online where people could listen to them, but it turned out that nobody really wanted to. The system itself was the artifact, not the clip that resulted from it. You couldn't break the project down into these separate pieces and talk about them on their own. It just doesn't work that way. It's a much more complicated ecology of production and expression.

But I'd like to go back to the scale question for a second. The interesting thing about scale is that, at a certain point, patterns begin to emerge. I think this is what Eric's work is all about, and he talked about the idea of emergence, about being able to see patterns and trends in the things being made. When the numbers

[53] KARAOKE ICE (2006), Remedios handing out free icy pops

are too small, it's much harder to see those patterns, which is why scale matters. I think that's why more and more of the work today is beginning to rely on data visualization as a way to help us see things that we can't normally see. It is becoming a tool for people to become creative within.

RODENBECK: **This reminds me of the moments on Digg when people are swarming around a story, and in the visualization you can observe the bubble representing that story grow. A few months ago there was a user revolt on Digg: people had posted stories containing an "illegal" piece of code that you could use to de-encode HD-DVD discs, and the stories had to be taken down because Digg was getting cease-and-desist letters from the record industry. The users on Digg decided that they really, really wanted this story on the site and kept putting it back up no matter how many times it was removed—basically they wouldn't take no for an answer and overwhelmed the site with postings. So we found ourselves in the interesting situation of having the visualizations on Digg Labs be the most visible indicator of the intense social upheaval that was going on. When we developed the visualizations, we had planned for a certain data rate to flow through, but during the revolt all of a sudden traffic just went through the roof. I think it was three times normal. And those nice gentle bubbles that you usually see floating in the visualizations were bouncing all over the place because the site was just going crazy.**
        With social media sites like Digg comes this culture that feeds back into itself and uses Digg to tell itself a story about its own values. The value of the site is not just about a single story or group of stories, it's about this whole ecology of users and the intense feelings of community they have about the site. It's not just about the

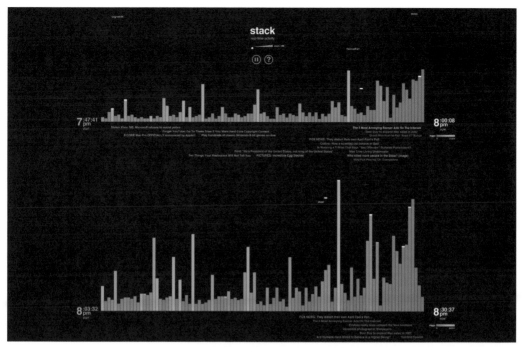

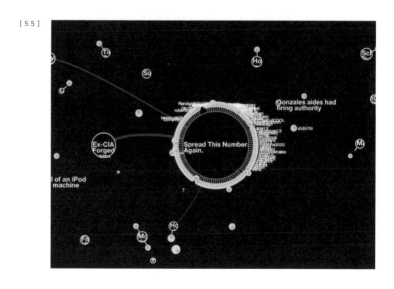

front page, and it's certainly not just about the clips after the karaoke that Katie was talking about earlier.

FRANK: My next question has to do with this kind of logarithmic curve that can be applied to a lot of different systems. It says that there's a small amount of people that are hyperactive, a few more people that are a little less active, and lots and lots of people that are barely active. Now, a comments box, which comes stock and standard with any of your blogs, doesn't pay any attention to those distinctions. It doesn't care whether you're a one-time user or a thousand-time user. So I'm wondering, do you talk differently to the squeaky wheel? To Terry T., or Tyler T., or whoever it is? Is there a kid that is running behind your karaoke truck, and do you have to come up with a few different models for different users? And then, in order to see patterns emerge, do you have to get rid of the big dots constantly? Does it become a pruning problem? Eric?

RODENBECK: The founder of Digg, Kevin Rose, is a bona fide rock star. Among the nerds, he's very well-known—people follow him around, and he's got a TV show. He's dating one of the Suicide Girls
and has all these fan boards devoted to what he does. So there's this phenomenon of people just digging everything that Kevin Rose diggs. He submits a story, and so many people are watching what he does and following him that five minutes later it's on the front page. In our visualization graphs you can see these patterns emerge. We actually do a lot of graphing that we don't make public. There's this cadre of people that just follow whatever any kind of celebrity posts, and this, of course, gets a little boring, because you think, "Well, Kevin posted that," so of course everybody's going

Laughs

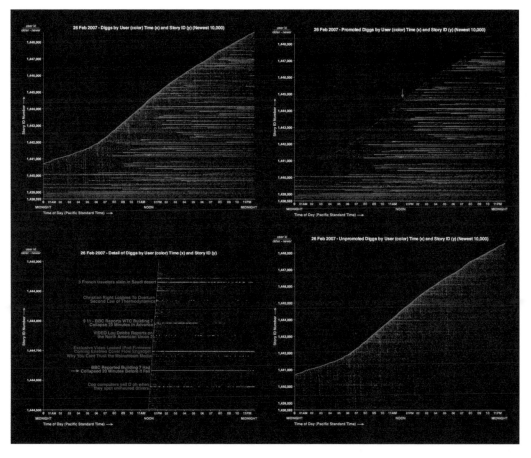

to comment on it. In our graphs we analyze this sort of thing and weed a lot of it out. But it's definitely a factor. At the same time, you want to encourage any kind of participation, because it's great that some five-year-old is following these stories even if it's only because a celebrity posted them.

For me controlling content is mainly about two things: removing vulgarity, obscene stuff, and building in mechanisms in the site that let the community police it, so that it's not necessarily just up to us, it's up to the people. If it's a well-functioning community, people that are antisocial get shunted into areas where they don't hurt anybody.

BUCHER: A site can create its own mini-celebrities, and that can give the project an extra boost. For example, there was one guy, Simon from Britain, who used to post on dailymonster.com all the time. Then, due to things that were happening in his real life, he had to stop posting for a little while. When he came back, I made it into a big event—the Return of Simon. And everybody said, "Oh, man, the Return of Simon, awesome." Do I deal with him and other frequent users differently? Only insofar as I have more offline contact with them, that I will email them personally more than I might somebody who is just a casual user. I try to keep them interested and forward them emails of people who tell me they loved their stories and so on. Emily, who posts some beautiful open-source monsters, is the rock star of that part of the site. People send me comments about her work, so I try to post them as often as I can.

Laughs   FRANK: Is she dating a Suicide Girl or anything like that?

Laughs   BUCHER: I don't know. She should.

FRANK: Stefan, your whole experience with the site, was this some purely idyllic thing? Was there anyone that said, "You know, this is so lame, I can't believe what you're doing?"

BUCHER: Only the Germans.

Laughs

FRANK: The Germans.

BUCHER: Yes, my people. The site was discussed on a blog in Germany that was run by Der Spiegel, the German equivalent of Newsweek. It was probably about a month-and-a-half in, and it was the first and only time that I got

Laughs

comments along the lines of "Pfft, I can do zat."

FRANK: Is that a German doing a fake German accent?

BUCHER: Yes, it's very meta, isn't it? To get back to your question, people said "Pfft, blowin' some ink around. That's not that hard." But other than that, it's been remarkably peaceful and good-willing. It's a California blog, so maybe that's why it's all so mellow.

FRANK: Before we move on to some questions from the audience, I would like you to talk a little about where you think this is headed, and where moments of interest are. Are we today in a special transitional economy, where kids who are thirteen don't actually give a crap about the distinction of whether something is consumer-generated or not, or whether it relies on Digg data or comes from Amazon? And to what extent can Dove post an amateur commercial during the Superbowl and people's reaction will be, "Psst, an amateur made it, it's cool," versus, "Whoa, Dove paid money for that?"

[58] BIRTH OF A MONSTER, poster for Lemon magazine, by Stefan G. Bucher, commissioned by Kevin Grady and Colin Metcalf

RODENBECK: I read an article in the <u>New York Times</u> recently about how dealing with user-generated content can turn out to be superexpensive. The actual process of managing and dealing with videos people submit to your site for use in some commercial or other, far from being a cost-saving way of doing things, can be hugely complicated: you have to deal with censorship issues, you have to deal with administrative issues, you have to deal with hosting issues. MoveOn.org, for example, had a Bush-in-thirty-seconds project where people could upload a thirty-second video that was going to be voted on by the MoveOn members. The plan was to put it online and air it during the Superbowl. But somebody submitted a video comparing Bush to Hitler and the right-wing media used that as an opportunity to denounce the organization. So tapping into the user community has risks associated with it.

BUCHER: It also has to do with the issue of scale you were touching on before. Are you doing it for your own personal enjoyment or are you acting on behalf of some larger agent?

FRANK: Like Hummer?

Laughs

BUCHER: I said **I'm sorry**.
Do you have to be responsible for some sort of larger entity and what effect your work has on them? Or is it just something that you're doing out of the privacy of your own home? Linked to that question is the issue of what your stated end goal is and whether you then have to police the project. Lastly, how much time are you asking people to invest? I'm basically asking for

[59-61] MOVEON.ORG LIVE MAPS. After the release of director Michael Moore's *Fahrenheit 9/11* in June 2004, MoveOn wanted to channel the excitement surrounding this movie into concrete action. Stamen developed a live, map-based, interactive Q&A session that allowed thousands of people to communicate visually via a moderated discussion.

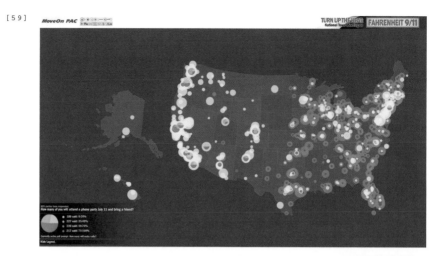

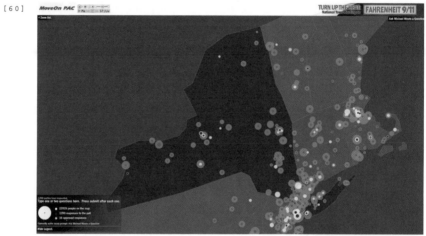

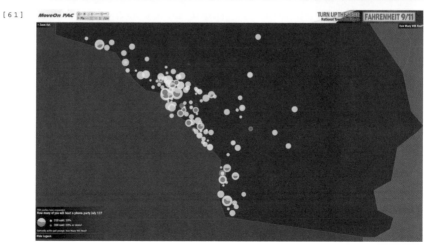

ninety seconds of your attention every couple of days. But a network comedy that needs to keep somebody interested for thirty minutes every week is a vastly more complicated task.

FRANK: Are we being pushed up the metachain, are we all going to be game designers, to some extent?

SALEN: I think what we're seeing today is a rising level of what I'll just call media literacy. People are more literate today in more media than they've ever been before. People learn how to write because they blog. They are learning about video editing and illustration and graphic design, so I think that there's a broader range of literacy across media. I don't think that that's going to change the fact that there will still be design professions. I don't think that there's a threat to the notion of mastery and craft in each of those professions. A way to look at it is that our language is being spoken by more people. It doesn't necessarily mean that all of those people are going to be incredibly fluent in it, or even that they need to be. But I do think that we're going to get rid of the concept of amateur—the notion of amateur-made content. Instead we may begin to think of it more as user-produced content, because the word amateur has a value judgment embedded within it. The term carries with it an idea that the work is not up to par, and that's not always the case. Sorry, that was a very convoluted answer!

Laughs

FRANK: Well, it was a convoluted question, so I appreciate it. Eric, did you have to add something?

RODENBECK: No, I'm writing down what she said so I can remember it later.

IT'S A TRUCK!!! STAY TUNED FOR...

KARAOKE ICE

FRANK: Oh, wow, Digg.

So does anyone have a question?

AUDIENCE MEMBER: Speaking about the future, I'm interested in the question of how to archive something like a blog successfully in a way that it is still usable and useful for future generations.

FRANK: Do you guys mind if I take one quick stab? When people move from other disciplines to the Internet, they often forget that their projects usually have an end. Online we tend to allow things to go on forever and expect that they can. But that's not the way the world works. You can only hold people's attention for so long. And if you allow a project to go past that point, it ends up as something that's filled with a bunch of conversations about conversations about conversations. It loses all contextual framing. So I think it's a dual challenge: One is knowing when to end, or at least keeping a time frame in mind when you do projects online that involve communities. And the other is taking a moment after the project is over to properly archive it, to tell the stories and point things in the right direction. To a certain extent you have to craft your own history because conversations, even at a dinner table, don't let themselves be archived very well.

SALEN: I think this is an excellent question because the issue of documentation is a huge one when you're doing this kind of work. You have to find a way to tell the story of what you think really happened in a project. It's an incredibly subjective task, because there's no way you can archive every little piece of data. That's where design really comes in—in the telling of the story, in the representation of what was interesting and meaningful about a particular project. That's where we go back to the traditional forms of the book, the poster, video, broadcast design, and so on. So work that may live in a dynamic, systemic medium initially often finds its way back into more easily archivable forms. Of course, there are people working on the problem of how to archive these kinds of projects, but I think in the end it comes back to taking a stab at trying to capture the experience for other people once a project is over. It comes back to communication. What is it that you want to say about this project, and how you can say that and share it with people?

BUCHER: I like to think about it this way: one form is a living landscape and the other is a picture of a landscape. Both can be enjoyable but in different ways. I'm doing a book about the first one hundred days of my site now, and I'm trying to figure out how to keep the content as entertaining in book format as it was online, where a large part of its appeal was the motion of the actual drawing and the particular sequence of the stories, their particular rhythm. How do you translate that into another medium?

FRANK: So it's really a different story altogether.

BUCHER: Yes, it is. In a way I feel like I'm doing what you're doing, Eric—I'm taking an existing data set and I'm processing it to crystallize different aspects for a new medium.

RODENBECK: I have two quick thoughts. I worked on a round-the-world sailing race in the late 1990s in San Francisco. For nine months we stayed up every night processing data and email and video and pictures, creating this whole compelling narrative about the sailing race. I thought it would be up forever. And then I left the company, and about two months later, the tech staff deleted that whole server before I had a chance to get any of the work off it, so nine months of some of the most exciting times of my life, which were absolutely fundamental to the way I now think and work, were suddenly just gone. I would love to be able to show what we created, because it meant a lot to me personally, but it's gone. So archive, totally archive, just archive!

Laughs

And the other thing is that nowadays all your emails and that sort of thing are still out there. Even if you deleted them from your in- or outbox, they're still somewhere in cyberspace. So that can work in your favor, too. You might not necessarily get a complete picture, but there will be bits and fragments. And maybe that's enough. How much paper ephemera do we really need? Of course, it's evocative because it's memory-generating, but I wonder whether a machine snapshot of your site is really every bit as evocative as the rest of it.

SALEN: Another important factor in participatory media is that the people who contributed have their own kind of archive of the experience as well. It's exponential: people post their stuff not just to your blog, but they have their own blog, too, on which they're posting. So there's this notion that your project lives in all of these people. It's being archived and reinvented and transformed in all of these different ways. That's what is so interesting about bringing the audience into the productive conversation. It just keeps going, it's like a living system.

RODENBECK: That's where the question of ownership also comes in.

FRANK: I think it is worth pointing out that all three of you developed communities and community platforms from scratch. But there're also a lot of interesting opportunities to work within existing platforms, such as Flickr, YouTube, or Facebook. Facebook, in particular, with its recent announcement of an application-building API, is going to be a massive playground for tons of projects. They have a community structure already set up, so they're very easy to just walk into and play around with.

Another question?

AUDIENCE MEMBER: I was wondering what your thoughts were on the relationship between the audience and the creator. Do you think that the role of the designer involves educating the audience whom he's inviting to participate to a certain extent? Because everybody who creates will become a designer in his or her own way. So does the role of designer involve creating the intended audience for your work, and establishing a platform for that audience to interact with?

RODENBECK: I think that this kind of interaction between designer and audience is going to be an increasing part of just the world in general. Forget about design. It's going to be a big part of what we all do. At Stamen we work with flows, and the people that we work with build platforms. But I think what is happening with platforms today is that they are starting to talk to each other, like Facebook and Flickr, for example. We're working on a project now that uses Facebook and Flickr at the same time. In this case you don't need to build the community from scratch, you don't need to educate the audience, because people are already using these existing networks. So these communities and platforms are becoming a landscape to be accreted on. There's soil now where there wasn't soil before. We can sift through it, and there are lots of different fertile places where things can grow. You still have to build, but there's a platform to build on.

BUCHER: I think there's a certain base inertia in all of us as well. There are things we like to participate in, but there's also a vast chunk of time when you just want to be given information to absorb, to be entertained, and be fairly passive. That kind of content still has to be provided. So I think it's an adjustment of percentages rather than a whole-scale revolution where ten years from now all we're going to do is design platforms for people to be wonderfully creative. If you look back at human history, that just doesn't seem to bear out.

FRANK: You could say that there was a parallel development in the Renaissance, the Enlightenment, and the Industrial Revolution. Certain tasks that seemed so at the core of design became automated. Hand lettering was replaced by casting and typesetting by hand, which was in turn replaced by the automated press, and so on. The business of design to some degree became about designing the machines that design. That's basically what book publishers are—they're metadesigners that design a completely different space. But the activity of making beautiful things, and the small niche audiences that appreciate these beautiful objects, still exist, regardless of the technology.

SALEN: Even within the gaming world this very debate is going on. In the past year people thought the wave of the future was to give the tools of the game over to the players to basically let them create their own games. But recently there's been this push-back by a number of game designers. Alexey Pajitnov, for example, the designer who created Tetris, developed a new game, and in an interview he was asked the question, "Why didn't you let the player design the levels of your game?" And he said, "Because I'm the designer." So even in game design, which is inherently participatory, there's a belief that sometimes you shouldn't give the players a chance to do everything that they might want to.

FRANK: We have time for one last question.

AUDIENCE MEMBER: I'd like to know what new projects you are currently working on.

SALEN: I am currently working on, or recently completed, several projects that involve audiences in highly participatory ways. The first, One Nature, premiered in Las Vegas on June 1, as part of an event known as First Friday. For this project Anfim Khanikov, an out-of-work Russian ice sculptor, dressed up in tuxedo and tails and wheeled a room service cart through the crowded sidewalks of the Las Vegas strip, accompanied by two formal waiters. He'd carved a small arctic landscape that sat atop the cart, absorbing the pavement heat, and invited passersby to indicate their degree of commitment in saving the environment by selecting a card from a customized deck. The cards were ordered by degree—0°, 1°, 180°, or 360°—and each card outlined the outcome of choosing to change one's environmental practices (or not). Khanikov commemorated each interaction with a "commitment ceremony," handing out wedding band–sized ice rings, cast from the meltwater of the iceberg carvings. So for a brief moment, the rings adorned those who chose to "become one" with nature.

The second, and most ambitious, project is the design of a new sixth- to twelfth-grade public school

[63-64] ONE NATURE (2007), a project by Katie Salen and Marina Zurkow, with Anfim Khanikov, in Las Vegas, Nevada

in New York City, themed around games and gaming. Opening in fall 2009, the school is being created by the Institute of Play, a not-for-profit organization I run that leverages games and play as transformative contexts for learning and creativity. All players in the school—teachers, students, parents, and administrators—will be empowered to innovate using twenty-first-century literacies that are native to games and design. This means learning to think about the world as a set of interconnected systems that can be affected or changed through action and choice, and developing the ability to navigate complex information networks, to build worlds and tell stories, to see collaboration in competition, and to communicate across diverse social spaces. It means that students and teachers will engage in their own learning in powerful ways. The school project casts the practice of designing audiences into a whole new light and one that I hope will be transformative for all.

RODENBECK: Something that I've been wanting to work on for some time now is a live data visualization that's more than just a view onto activity that is happening elsewhere. I want it to also serve as an interface through which users can manipulate the underlying data, so they can reach through the display into what it is representing and explore a different kind of possibility space instead of just watching what other people are doing. We're also working on customized views that are specific to a user's interests and network activity, and on finding better ways to let people link to specific parts of the experiences so that they can share them more easily. In another project we're using some of the lessons we've learned from the social-networking world to shed light on less Internet-specific social and civic spaces. States and cities generate data all the time as a matter of

[65-66] 344 ONLINE STORE, by Stefan G. Bucher

course, but don't necessarily have a good way of sharing it with the public. We've started to take a close look at the way crime and police work is represented, as well as how congressional politics works with earmarking and things like that. One of the interesting things about this kind of work, especially on the national level, is that there are a lot of people who have a vested interest in hiding behind a status quo where the public can't easily understand what's going on behind the scenes. We'd like to change that, especially since the 2008 presidential election could be a chance to change the direction the country is going in. We want to be a part of change in the real world as well as on the Internet, and hope that visualization can play a key role in helping people to better understand the world they live in.

BUCHER: I'm continuing to evolve dailymonster.com to keep it a fun and interesting site for people to visit and play with. I'm working on my books, of course, and on a number of little monster-related products for the online store. It's an experiment to see if I can break out of the service sector and make a living as a sort of attention-deficit artisan. When people ask me to define my style, I usually call it "gratuitously ambitious." Which is true. It's ambitious when it doesn't necessarily have to be, but the more I do work that I'm really crazy about, the more I seem to attract kindred spirits that want to work with me on their own dream projects. I'm always surprised—both in terms of my clients and the people who contribute to the site—how much passionate energy for good is out there. If I can help people focus that energy, that's a good day at the office.

FRANK: Thanks everyone, and thank you for coming.

Applause

www.344design.com

www.stamen.com

www.zefrank.com

Thank you for your participation!